How to Start and Grow Your Own Trucking Business

The Foolproof Plan to Kickstart Your Trucking Company Success!

Content

18. Establishing and maintaining compliance with safety regulations
19. Understanding and managing fuel costs
20. Building and managing an effective dispatch and routing system
21. Developing a marketing strategy for your trucking business
22. Understanding and managing fuel costs
23. Building and maintaining a fleet maintenance program
24. Managing and reducing turnover among drivers and staff
25. Utilizing social media and online tools to promote your business
26. Understanding and managing taxes and accounting
27. Improving customer service and building a loyal customer base
28. Understanding and managing cash flow and financial forecasting
29. Developing a strategy for recruiting and retaining drivers
30. Building and maintaining a safety culture within your company
31. Navigating the legal landscape of the trucking industry
32. Utilizing telematics and other technology to improve productivity
33. Building and maintaining relationships with other businesses in the supply chain

34. Understanding the role of freight brokers and how to work with them
35. Mastering negotiation and pricing strategies
36. Understanding and managing fuel costs
37. Building and maintaining a culture of continuous improvement
38. Managing and reducing downtime and lost productivity
39. Understanding and managing employee benefits and payroll
40. Planning for the future: Continual growth and expansion of your trucking business.

Introduction

Welcome to the world of trucking! As a trucking entrepreneur, you're about to embark on a journey that can be both challenging and rewarding. The trucking industry is a vital part of the global economy, and as a trucking business owner, you'll play a key role in keeping goods and products moving from place to place. In this chapter, we'll give you a comprehensive introduction to the trucking industry, including its history, current state, and future trends.

The History of Trucking:

Trucking has been around for over a century, with the first motorized delivery vehicles appearing on the roads in the early 1900s. However, it wasn't until the 1920s and 1930s that trucking began to take off as a major industry. With the growth of manufacturing and the rise of consumerism, more and more goods needed to be transported from one place to another. The trucking industry was there to meet that demand, and it has continued to grow and evolve ever since.

The Current State of the Industry:

Today, the trucking industry is a massive and diverse sector of the economy. According to the American Trucking Association, the trucking industry generates over $800 billion in revenue annually and employs more than 7 million people. The industry moves over 71% of all freight transported in the United States and plays a vital role in the global economy. The trucking industry is also constantly evolving, with new technologies and trends emerging all the time.

Future Trends:

There are a few key trends that are likely to shape the trucking industry in the coming years. One of the biggest is the increasing use of technology, with many trucking companies now using telematics and other tools to improve efficiency and productivity. Another trend is the growing demand for "green" or environmentally friendly trucking, as more and more companies look to reduce their carbon footprint. Finally, the trucking industry is facing a shortage of drivers, which is likely to become more acute as the economy continues to recover.

Conclusion:

The trucking industry is a vital part of the global economy and offers many opportunities for entrepreneurs. By understanding its history, current state, and future trends, you can better position yourself to succeed in the trucking business. With hard work, dedication and a good business plan, you can grow your business and make it a success.

Understanding the costs and financial requirements of starting a trucking business

Starting a trucking business can be a significant investment, both in terms of time and money. In this chapter, we'll take a detailed look at the costs and financial requirements associated with starting a trucking business, so you can make informed decisions about whether this is the right business for you.

Initial Costs:

The initial costs of starting a trucking business can vary widely depending on the size and scope of your business. Some of the most significant expenses include:

- Trucks and equipment: Depending on the type of trucking business you're starting, you may need to purchase or lease a fleet of trucks, trailers, and other equipment. This can be one of the biggest expenses associated with starting a trucking business and can range from tens of thousands to hundreds of thousands of dollars.
- Insurance: All trucking businesses are required to have liability insurance to protect against potential accidents and damage. The cost of insurance can vary depending on the size of your fleet and the type of cargo you're transporting.
- Licenses and permits: Depending on the state or states where you operate, you may need to obtain various licenses and permits to legally operate your trucking business. These can include commercial driver's

licenses, federal motor carrier authority, and state-specific permits.
- Office space and equipment: You'll also need to budget for office space and equipment, such as computers, phones, and software.
- Staffing: If you plan to hire employees, you'll need to budget for salaries and benefits.

Ongoing Costs:

In addition to the initial costs, there are also ongoing costs associated with running a trucking business. Some of the most significant expenses include:

- Fuel: Fuel is one of the biggest expenses associated with running a trucking business and can fluctuate widely depending on the price of oil.
- Maintenance and repairs: Keeping your trucks and equipment in good working order can be a significant expense, especially if you have a large fleet.
- Insurance: As mentioned earlier, insurance is a requirement for trucking businesses and need to be budgeted for on an ongoing basis.
- Taxes: As a business owner, you'll be responsible for paying federal and state taxes on your business income.
- Staffing: If you have employees, you'll need to budget for salaries, benefits, and other related costs.

Financial Requirements:

Starting a trucking business requires a significant amount of capital. Many entrepreneurs will rely on a combination of personal savings, loans from banks or other lenders, and investments from friends and family to finance their business. Some other options include leasing equipment, renting a fleet, or using a fleet management company.

It's important to remember that starting a trucking business is a long-term investment and you should be prepared for the unexpected costs and expenses that may arise. It is also crucial to have a solid business plan that outlines how you plan to generate revenue and make a profit.

Conclusion: Starting a trucking business can be a significant investment, both in terms of time and money, but it can also be a rewarding and profitable venture. By understanding the costs and financial requirements associated with starting a trucking business, you can make informed decisions about whether this is the right business for you. It's also important to have a solid business plan and to be prepared for unexpected costs and expenses. With the right planning, you can successfully start and grow your own trucking business.

Developing a Business Plan for Your Trucking Company

A business plan is a vital tool for any entrepreneur, and this is especially true when starting a trucking business. A well-written business plan will help you to clearly define your business goals, identify potential challenges, and outline the steps you'll need to take to achieve success.

Here are some key elements to include in your business plan:

1. Executive Summary: This section should provide a brief overview of your business, including your company's mission statement, goals, and target market.
2. Industry Analysis: This section should provide an overview of the trucking industry, including the size of the market, major players, trends, and opportunities.
3. Market Analysis: In this section, you'll need to research and analyze your target market, including the demographics of your customers and the type of cargo you'll be transporting.
4. Operations and Logistics: This section should detail how your trucking business will operate, including the types of trucks and equipment you'll need, your routing and scheduling, and your logistics strategy.
5. Sales and Marketing: This section should detail your sales and marketing strategy, including how you plan to generate leads and convert them into customers.
6. Financial Projections: This section should include financial projections, such as projected revenue, expenses, and profitability.

7. Management and Staffing: This section should detail the management structure of your business and your staffing needs, including the roles and responsibilities of each employee.
8. Conclusion: Sum up your business plan, and provide a summary of your main objectives, strategies, and projected results.

Tips for Writing Your Business Plan:

1. Be clear and concise: Keep your business plan to a manageable length, and make sure that the language you use is easy to understand.
2. Be realistic: Your business plan should be based on solid research and realistic assumptions.
3. Be prepared: Make sure that you have all the information you need to complete your business plan before you begin writing.
4. Get feedback: Share your business plan with friends, family, and industry experts, and take their feedback into account when making revisions.
5. Review and revise: A business plan is not a one-time document, it's a living document, review it regularly and make the necessary updates to keep it relevant.

Conclusion: A business plan is a vital tool for any entrepreneur, and this is especially true when starting a trucking business. A well-written business plan will help you to clearly define your business goals, identify potential challenges, and outline the steps you'll need to take to achieve success. By following the tips provided in this chapter, you can develop a solid business plan that will help guide your trucking business on the path to success.

Securing Funding for Your Trucking Business

Starting a trucking business can be a costly endeavor, and securing funding is an important step in getting your business up and running. There are several options available to entrepreneurs looking to secure funding, each with its own advantages and disadvantages.

Here are some common options for funding your trucking business:

1. Personal savings: Using your own savings is a great way to get your business off the ground, as it eliminates the need to pay interest or give up equity in your company.
2. Small Business Administration (SBA) loans: The SBA offers a variety of loan programs, including the 7(a) loan program, which is specifically designed to help small businesses secure funding.
3. Business credit cards: Business credit cards can provide a convenient way to finance your trucking business, but it's important to be aware of the potential drawbacks, including high interest rates and fees.
4. Angel investors: Angel investors are individuals who are willing to invest their own money in your business in exchange for equity.
5. Crowdfunding: Crowdfunding is a way of raising money by asking a large number of people for small amounts of money.
6. Leasing: Leasing equipment, such as trucks, trailers, and other vehicles, is another way to secure financing.

Tips for Securing Funding:

1. Create a detailed business plan: A well-written business plan will help you to clearly define your business goals, identify potential challenges, and outline the steps you'll need to take to achieve success. This will help you to secure funding by showing lenders, investors, or crowdfunding sites that your business is a viable investment.
2. Build your credit: A good credit score can make it easier to secure funding, so make sure that you take steps to build your credit before applying for a loan or credit card.
3. Do your research: Research the different funding options available, and choose the one that best suits your needs.
4. Network: Network with other entrepreneurs, business owners, and investors in your community. You never know who might be able to connect you with potential funding sources.
5. Be prepared: Make sure that you have all the information you need to complete your funding application before you begin. This includes financial statements, tax returns, and other relevant documents.

Conclusion: Starting a trucking business can be a costly endeavor, and securing funding is an important step in getting your business up and running. There are several options available to entrepreneurs looking to secure funding, each with its own advantages and disadvantages. By following the tips provided in this chapter, you can identify the best funding options for your trucking business and increase your chances of securing the funding you need to get your business up and running.

Choosing the Right Type of Truck and Equipment for Your Business

When starting a trucking business, one of the most important decisions you'll have to make is choosing the right type of truck and equipment for your business. This decision will depend on a variety of factors, including the types of goods you'll be transporting, the distance you'll be traveling, and the size of your business.

Here are some things to consider when choosing the right type of truck and equipment for your business:

1. Type of cargo: The type of cargo you'll be transporting will play a big role in determining the type of truck and equipment you'll need. For example, if you'll be transporting hazardous materials, you'll need a truck that is equipped with special safety features.
2. Distance traveled: The distance you'll be traveling will also play a role in determining the type of truck and equipment you'll need. If you'll be making long hauls, you'll need a truck that is designed for long-distance travel.
3. Size of your business: The size of your business will also play a role in determining the type of truck and equipment you'll need. If you're just starting out, you may want to consider leasing a truck rather than buying one outright.
4. Fuel efficiency: Fuel efficiency is a crucial factor to consider when choosing a truck and equipment for your business. The cost of fuel can add up quickly, so it's important to choose a truck and equipment that will save you money on fuel in the long run.

5. Maintenance and repair costs: The cost of maintaining and repairing your truck and equipment is another important factor to consider. Make sure to choose a truck and equipment that will be easy to maintain and repair.

Tips for Choosing the Right Type of Truck and Equipment:

1. Do your research: Research the different types of trucks and equipment available, and choose the ones that best suit your business needs.
2. Test drive: Take the time to test drive different trucks and equipment before making a decision. This will give you a better sense of how they handle and perform.
3. Get a mechanic's opinion: Before purchasing a truck or equipment, have a mechanic inspect it to ensure that it is in good condition.
4. Look for warranty and maintenance packages: Many truck and equipment manufacturers offer warranty and maintenance packages that can help to protect your investment.
5. Compare prices: Compare prices from different dealers to ensure that you're getting the best deal.

Conclusion: Choosing the right type of truck and equipment for your business is a crucial decision that will have a big impact on your business's success. By considering the type of cargo you'll be transporting, the distance you'll be traveling, the size of your business, fuel efficiency, and maintenance and repair costs, you can make an informed decision that will help your business to thrive. Remember to do your research, test drive and have a mechanic inspect the truck and equipment, look for warranty and maintenance packages, and compare prices from different dealers to ensure that you're getting the best deal.

Understanding and Complying with Federal and State Regulations

When starting a trucking business, it's important to understand and comply with all federal and state regulations. These regulations cover a wide range of issues, including vehicle safety, driver qualifications, and environmental protection.

Here are some of the key federal and state regulations that you'll need to be aware of:

1. Federal Motor Carrier Safety Administration (FMCSA): The FMCSA is responsible for regulating the trucking industry at the federal level. They have regulations in place for everything from driver qualifications to vehicle safety.
2. Department of Transportation (DOT): The DOT is responsible for enforcing federal transportation regulations. They have regulations in place for things like hours of service, drug and alcohol testing, and vehicle inspection.
3. Environmental Protection Agency (EPA): The EPA is responsible for enforcing federal environmental regulations. They have regulations in place for things like emissions and fuel efficiency.
4. State regulations: Each state also has their own set of regulations that you'll need to comply with. These can vary from state to state, so it's important to be aware of the regulations in the states where you'll be operating.

Tips for Complying with Federal and State Regulations:

1. Stay informed: Keep up to date with changes to federal and state regulations. The FMCSA and other agencies often update regulations, so it's important to stay informed.
2. Have a compliance plan: Develop a plan for how you'll comply with federal and state regulations. This plan should include things like regular vehicle inspections and driver training.
3. Keep accurate records: Keep accurate records of things like vehicle inspections and driver qualifications. This will help you to comply with regulations and prove compliance if necessary.
4. Hire a compliance officer: Consider hiring a compliance officer to help you stay on top of regulations.
5. Consult with industry experts: Consulting with industry experts, such as trucking industry lawyer or consultant, can help you to navigate the regulations and ensure compliance.

Conclusion: Complying with federal and state regulations is an important part of operating a trucking business. By understanding the regulations in place and developing a plan for how you'll comply with them, you can ensure that your business is operating legally and safely. Stay informed, have a compliance plan, keep accurate records, hire a compliance officer and consulting with industry experts can help you to navigate the regulations and ensure compliance.

Hiring and Managing Drivers and Staff

As a trucking business owner, one of the most important aspects of your business will be hiring and managing drivers and staff. Having the right drivers and staff in place is crucial to the success of your business. They are the face of your company, and their actions and performance will directly impact your business's reputation and bottom line.

Here are some tips for hiring and managing drivers and staff:

1. Hiring: When hiring drivers, look for individuals with a good driving record, a clean background check, and the proper qualifications. Be sure to thoroughly check references and conduct a thorough interview process.
2. Training: Once you've hired drivers, be sure to provide them with proper training. This can include training on safety procedures, federal and state regulations, and company policies and procedures.
3. Monitoring and evaluation: Regularly monitor and evaluate the performance of your drivers and staff. This can include things like monitoring their driving record, their compliance with regulations, and their customer service skills.
4. Communication: Encourage open and clear communication between drivers and staff and management. This can help to build trust and ensure that everyone is working together towards the same goals.
5. Recognition and rewards: Recognize and reward good performance. This can help to motivate and retain your drivers and staff.

6. Safety: Prioritize safety and compliance by encouraging your drivers and staff to report any unsafe driving practices or violations, and ensure that they are aware of all the safety guidelines and regulations to follow.
7. Support and development: Offer support and development opportunities to your drivers and staff. This can include things like additional training or cross-training to help them advance in their careers.

Conclusion: Hiring and managing drivers and staff is crucial to the success of your trucking business. By hiring the right individuals, providing proper training, monitoring and evaluating performance, encouraging open communication, recognizing and rewarding good performance, prioritizing safety and compliance and offering support and development opportunities, you can help to build a strong and effective team that will help your business to thrive.

Building and Maintaining a Positive Reputation and Brand for Your Business

In today's competitive marketplace, having a positive reputation and brand is crucial for the success of your trucking business. Your reputation and brand can impact everything from attracting new customers to retaining existing ones, and it's important to take the time to build and maintain a positive reputation and brand for your business.

Here are some tips for building and maintaining a positive reputation and brand for your business:

1. Deliver quality service: The most important aspect of building a positive reputation and brand is to deliver quality service to your customers. This can include things like timely delivery, excellent customer service, and an overall positive experience.
2. Be responsive: Be responsive to your customers' needs and concerns. This can include things like responding quickly to customer complaints or providing updates on delivery status.
3. Use social media: Take advantage of social media to build and maintain a positive reputation and brand. Use platforms like Facebook, Twitter, and LinkedIn to engage with customers, share information about your business, and build a community around your brand.
4. Be consistent: Be consistent in your messaging and branding. This can help to build trust and credibility with your customers.
5. Be transparent: Be transparent about your business practices and policies. This can help to build trust and credibility with your customers.

6. Encourage customer feedback: Encourage customer feedback and be open to suggestions for improvement. This can help you identify areas where you can improve your service and build a stronger reputation.
7. Get involved in the community: Get involved in your local community. This can include things like sponsoring local events or participating in community service projects.
8. Partner with other businesses: Partner with other businesses to promote your brand and reputation. This can include things like cross-promotions or co-branding opportunities.

Conclusion: Building and maintaining a positive reputation and brand for your trucking business is essential for success. By delivering quality service, being responsive, using social media, being consistent, transparent, and encourage customer feedback, getting involved in the community and partnering with other businesses, you can build a positive reputation and brand that will help your business to thrive.

Understanding and Managing Logistics and Operations

In order to run a successful trucking business, it's essential to have a solid understanding of logistics and operations. This includes everything from managing routes and schedules, to tracking inventory and shipments, to ensuring compliance with federal regulations.

Here are some tips for understanding and managing logistics and operations in your trucking business:

1. Plan your routes: One of the most important aspects of logistics and operations is planning efficient routes for your trucks. This can include things like avoiding heavy traffic areas, choosing the most fuel-efficient routes, and taking into account weather conditions.
2. Use technology: Technology can help you manage logistics and operations more effectively. Consider using software to track inventory and shipments, plan routes, and schedule deliveries.
3. Monitor compliance: It's important to stay compliant with federal regulations when it comes to logistics and operations. This can include things like monitoring driver hours, maintaining accurate records, and ensuring that your trucks and equipment are in compliance with safety regulations.
4. Communicate effectively: Good communication is key when it comes to logistics and operations. Make sure that your drivers and staff are aware of any changes to routes or schedules, and that they have the necessary information to complete their deliveries.

5. Be flexible: Be prepared to adapt to unexpected changes in logistics and operations. This can include things like traffic delays or weather-related issues.
6. Optimize your fleet: Optimize your fleet for maximum efficiency. This can include things like using GPS tracking, implementing route optimization software, and regularly maintaining your trucks and equipment.
7. Utilize third-party logistics providers: Utilize third-party logistics providers (3PL) to help manage logistics and operations. 3PLs can provide services such as warehousing, transportation, and distribution.
8. Keep track of your inventory: Keep track of your inventory, by using tools such as barcode scanning, RFID, or warehouse management systems. This will help you to manage your inventory more effectively and improve customer service.

Conclusion: Managing logistics and operations is an essential part of running a successful trucking business. By planning your routes, using technology, monitoring compliance, communicating effectively, being flexible, optimizing your fleet, utilizing third-party logistics providers, and keeping track of your inventory, you can manage logistics and operations more effectively and improve the overall performance of your business.

Building a network of clients and customers

One of the most important aspects of running a successful trucking business is building a strong network of clients and customers. This includes finding and building relationships with potential customers, as well as maintaining and growing those relationships over time.

Here are some tips for building a network of clients and customers in your trucking business:

1. Identify your target market: The first step in building a network of clients and customers is to identify your target market. This can include things like the types of goods you will be transporting, the industries you will be serving, and the geographic areas you will be covering.
2. Network and market yourself: Once you have identified your target market, it's important to network and market yourself to potential customers. This can include things like attending trade shows, joining industry associations, and attending networking events.
3. Use online marketing: Online marketing is a powerful tool for building a network of clients and customers. This can include things like creating a website, using social media, and implementing search engine optimization (SEO) strategies.
4. Leverage referrals: Leverage referrals to grow your network of clients and customers. Encourage current customers to refer their friends and colleagues to your business.

5. Develop a strong sales pitch: Develop a strong sales pitch that highlights the benefits of your trucking services and how they can help potential customers.
6. Offer exceptional customer service: Offer exceptional customer service to your clients and customers. This can include things like being responsive to customer needs, providing regular updates on shipments, and addressing any issues or concerns in a timely manner.
7. Build long-term relationships: Building long-term relationships with clients and customers is key to the success of your trucking business. This can include things like offering loyalty programs, creating customer appreciation events, and regularly checking in with customers to see how you can continue to meet their needs.
8. Negotiate rates and contracts: Negotiate rates and contracts with your clients and customers. This will help to establish long-term relationships and create a sustainable business model.

Conclusion: Building a network of clients and customers is essential for the success of your trucking business. By identifying your target market, networking and marketing yourself, using online marketing, leveraging referrals, developing a strong sales pitch, offering exceptional customer service, building long-term relationships, and negotiating rates and contracts, you can create a strong network of clients and customers that will help to drive the growth and success of your business.

Using Technology to Improve Efficiency and Productivity

Technology has the power to revolutionize the trucking industry, making it more efficient and productive than ever before. From GPS tracking and dispatch software to electronic logging devices and telematics, there are a wide variety of technological tools and solutions available to trucking businesses.

Here are some ways that technology can be used to improve efficiency and productivity in your trucking business:

1. GPS tracking and dispatch software: GPS tracking and dispatch software allows you to track the location and movement of your vehicles in real-time, making it easier to plan routes, manage drivers, and ensure timely deliveries.
2. Electronic logging devices: Electronic logging devices (ELDs) are required by federal regulations for commercial truck drivers, and they help to ensure compliance with hours of service rules and regulations.
3. Telematics: Telematics systems provide real-time data on things like fuel consumption, vehicle performance, and driver behavior, allowing you to identify areas where efficiency can be improved and make necessary changes.
4. Mobile apps and web portals: Mobile apps and web portals allow drivers and dispatchers to access important information and communicate with each other while on the road.
5. Automation of paperwork: Automation of paperwork such as invoicing, billing, and record keeping can save time and reduce the risk of errors.

6. Automated vehicle maintenance: Automated vehicle maintenance systems help to ensure that your vehicles are always in good working condition, reducing the risk of breakdowns and downtime.
7. Artificial intelligence and machine learning: Artificial intelligence and machine learning can be used to optimize routes, predict maintenance needs, and even assist with driver recruiting and retention.
8. Cloud-based solutions: Cloud-based solutions allow you to access important data and information from anywhere, making it easier to manage your business remotely.

Conclusion: Technology has the power to revolutionize the trucking industry, making it more efficient and productive than ever before. By using tools such as GPS tracking and dispatch software, electronic logging devices, telematics, mobile apps, automation of paperwork, automated vehicle maintenance, artificial intelligence and machine learning, and cloud-based solutions, you can improve the efficiency and productivity of your trucking business, and stay ahead of the competition. Keep in mind that while technology can be a powerful tool, it's important to balance its use with human interaction as well.

Managing and Reducing Risk in Your Trucking Business

Managing and reducing risk is an important aspect of running a successful trucking business. There are a variety of risks that trucking businesses face, from accidents and breakdowns to legal disputes and financial losses. By taking steps to manage and reduce risk, you can protect your business and ensure its long-term success.

Here are some ways that you can manage and reduce risk in your trucking business:

1. Compliance with regulations: Compliance with federal and state regulations is essential for reducing risk in the trucking industry. This includes compliance with safety regulations, hours of service rules, and environmental regulations.
2. Risk management training: Risk management training can help your drivers and staff understand the risks they may face and how to avoid them.
3. Insurance: Insurance is an essential tool for managing and reducing risk in the trucking industry. This includes liability insurance, cargo insurance, and insurance for your vehicles and equipment.
4. Maintenance: Regular maintenance of your vehicles and equipment can help to reduce the risk of breakdowns and accidents.
5. Safety programs: Safety programs can help to reduce the risk of accidents and injuries. This includes driver training, safety incentives, and regular safety audits.
6. Risk assessment and analysis: Regular risk assessment and analysis can help to identify potential risks and take steps to mitigate them.

7. Communication and coordination: Good communication and coordination between drivers, dispatchers, and other staff can help to avoid misunderstandings and mistakes that could lead to accidents or delays.
8. Crisis management: Developing a crisis management plan can help to minimize the impact of an accident or other emergency.

Conclusion: Managing and reducing risk is an important aspect of running a successful trucking business. By taking steps such as compliance with regulations, risk management training, insurance, maintenance, safety programs, risk assessment and analysis, communication and coordination, and crisis management, you can protect your business and ensure its long-term success. Keep in mind that trucking business is a high-risk industry, so it's important to be aware of potential risks and take proactive steps to mitigate them.

Understanding and managing insurance and liability

Understanding and Managing Insurance and Liability in Your Trucking Business:

Insurance and liability are critical components of managing risk in the trucking industry. As a trucking business owner, it's essential to understand the types of insurance that are available to you and how they can protect your business from financial loss.

Here are some key types of insurance that trucking businesses should consider:

1. Liability insurance: Liability insurance protects your business from financial loss in the event that you or one of your drivers causes an accident or damage. It covers the cost of legal defense and any settlements or judgments that may result from a lawsuit.
2. Cargo insurance: Cargo insurance covers the loss or damage of the goods you're transporting. This is especially important if you're transporting high-value goods, as the cost of replacing them can be substantial.
3. Physical damage insurance: Physical damage insurance covers the cost of repairing or replacing your vehicles and equipment in the event of an accident or other damage.
4. Non-trucking liability insurance: Non-trucking liability insurance covers the cost of any accidents or damage that occur when your truck is not being used for business purposes.
5. Workers' compensation insurance: Workers' compensation insurance covers the cost of medical

treatment and lost wages for employees who are injured on the job.

6. Occupational Accident Insurance: Occupational Accident Insurance covers the cost of medical treatment and lost wages for drivers who are injured on the job.

It's important to note that the insurance requirements for trucking businesses vary by state, so it's essential to check with your state's Department of Transportation for specific requirements.

When choosing an insurance policy, it's important to work with an experienced insurance agent who understands the unique risks and needs of the trucking industry. They can help you to identify the coverage you need and find the most cost-effective policies.

In addition to insurance, it's important to have a liability management plan in place to minimize the risk of accidents and financial losses. This includes regular driver training, safety incentives, and regular safety audits.

Conclusion: Insurance and liability are critical components of managing risk in the trucking industry. As a trucking business owner, it's essential to understand the types of insurance that are available to you and how they can protect your business from financial loss. Work with an experienced insurance agent to identify the coverage you need, and implement a liability management plan to minimize the risk of accidents and financial losses. Remember to check with your state's Department of Transportation for specific requirements.

Staying current with industry trends and changes

Staying Current with Industry Trends and Changes in the Trucking Business:

The trucking industry is constantly evolving, and as a business owner, it's essential to stay current with the latest trends and changes. Keeping up with industry developments can help you to stay competitive, increase efficiency and productivity, and grow your business.

Here are some key trends and changes to keep an eye on in the trucking industry:

1. E-commerce and online shopping: The growth of e-commerce is increasing the demand for trucking services as more goods are being delivered directly to consumers. As a trucking business, it's essential to understand how e-commerce trends are impacting your business and how to adapt your services to meet the changing needs of your customers.
2. Automation and technology: Automation and technology are playing an increasingly important role in the trucking industry. From self-driving trucks to logistics software, these advancements are helping to improve efficiency and reduce costs. As a business owner, it's important to stay current with the latest technology and consider how it can benefit your business.
3. Government regulations: The trucking industry is heavily regulated, and changes in laws and regulations can have a significant impact on your business. It's essential to stay current with the latest regulations,

including new safety standards and compliance requirements.

4. Environmental concerns: The trucking industry has been facing increasing pressure to reduce emissions and be more environmentally friendly. As a business owner, it's important to understand these concerns and consider how to reduce your environmental impact.

5. Shortage of drivers: The industry is facing a shortage of drivers, this can cause delays and make it difficult to find reliable and qualified drivers. As a business owner, it's important to stay informed about the driver shortage and consider how it will impact your business.

6. Electric and hybrid vehicles: The industry is slowly shifting towards electric and hybrid vehicles, this could mean a lot of changes in the industry, from charging infrastructure to regulations.

One way to stay current with industry trends and changes is to join a professional trucking association or attend industry conferences and events. These organizations and events provide valuable networking opportunities, as well as access to the latest information and resources.

It's also important to stay in touch with your customers and suppliers, as they can provide valuable insights into how industry trends and changes are impacting their businesses.

Conclusion: The trucking industry is constantly evolving, and as a business owner, it's essential to stay current with the latest trends and changes. Keeping up with industry developments can help you to stay competitive, increase efficiency and productivity, and grow your business. Join professional trucking association, attend industry conferences, stay in touch with your customers and suppliers, and stay informed about the latest regulations. This will help you to stay current with industry trends and changes.

Scaling your business and expanding operations

Once your trucking business is established and profitable, you may want to consider scaling your operations and expanding your business. Growing your business can help you to increase revenue and profits, gain market share, and create new opportunities for growth.

Here are some tips for scaling your trucking business and expanding your operations:

1. Review your business plan: Before you begin expanding your operations, it's essential to review your business plan and ensure that your business is in a position to scale. You'll need to have a solid financial foundation, a strong team in place, and a clear vision for the future of your business.
2. Identify new revenue streams: Look for new revenue streams that you can tap into to help drive your business forward. This might include expanding into new markets, offering new services, or developing new products.
3. Invest in technology: Technology can be a powerful tool for scaling your business and increasing efficiency. Investing in logistics software, GPS tracking, and other technologies can help you to improve your operations, reduce costs, and increase productivity.
4. Hire more drivers and staff: As your business grows, you'll need to hire more drivers and staff to keep up with the increased demand for your services. It's essential to have a strong recruitment and training program in place to attract and retain the best drivers and staff.

5. Expand your fleet: As your business grows, you may need to expand your fleet of trucks and equipment to meet the increased demand for your services. This might involve purchasing new trucks or leasing additional equipment.
6. Build a strong network: Building a strong network of clients, suppliers, and partners is essential for scaling your business and expanding your operations. This can help you to secure new business, expand into new markets, and build your reputation as a reliable and trustworthy trucking company.
7. Monitor and track your progress: It's essential to monitor and track your progress as you scale your business and expand your operations. This will help you to identify any challenges or obstacles, as well as opportunities for growth.
8. Seek professional advice: It's always a good idea to seek professional advice when scaling your business and expanding your operations. Consult with a business coach, accountant, or lawyer to help you navigate the challenges of growth and ensure that your business is on the right track.

Conclusion: Scaling your business and expanding your operations is a significant step for any trucking business. It's essential to have a solid financial foundation, a strong team in place, and a clear vision for the future of your business. Identify new revenue streams, invest in technology, hire more drivers and staff, expand your fleet, build a strong network, monitor and track your progress, and seek professional advice to help you navigate the challenges of growth. This will help you to ensure that your business is on the right track for scaling and expanding.

Using Data and Analytics to Make Informed Business Decisions

In today's fast-paced business world, data and analytics are crucial tools for making informed decisions. In the trucking industry, data and analytics can be used to track and analyze a wide range of metrics, including fuel consumption, vehicle performance, and driver productivity. By using these tools, you can gain valuable insights into your business operations and identify areas where improvements can be made.

To get started with data and analytics, you'll need to set up a system for collecting and storing data. This can be as simple as using a spreadsheet or a more advanced tool such as a dedicated fleet management software. You'll also need to establish key performance indicators (KPIs) that you want to track and measure. Some examples of KPIs for a trucking business include:

- Fleet utilization: How much of your fleet is being used and how much is sitting idle?
- Fuel efficiency: How much fuel is your fleet consuming and what is the average miles per gallon?
- Driver performance: How many miles are your drivers logging each day and how many accidents have they been involved in?
- Maintenance costs: How much are you spending on maintenance and repairs for your fleet?

Once you have your data collection and storage system in place and your KPIs identified, you can start analyzing the data to gain insights into your business. For example, if you notice that your fleet utilization is low, you may want to consider ways to increase the number of loads your trucks are carrying. Or, if you find that your fuel efficiency is low, you may want to investigate ways to improve vehicle performance or reduce idling time.

Another important aspect of data and analytics is data visualization. This refers to the process of creating charts, graphs, and other visual representations of data to help you easily understand and communicate key insights. By using data visualization tools, you can identify patterns and trends that may not be immediately apparent from raw data.

In addition to tracking internal metrics, it's also important to stay up-to-date with industry trends and changes. This can be done by subscribing to trade publications, attending industry conferences, and networking with other trucking business owners. By staying current with industry trends and changes, you'll be better equipped to make informed business decisions that will help your business grow and thrive.

In conclusion, data and analytics are powerful tools that can help you gain a deeper understanding of your business operations and make informed decisions. By setting up a system for collecting and storing data, identifying key performance indicators, and using data visualization tools, you'll be well on your way to using data and analytics to improve your trucking business.

Building and Maintaining Positive Relationships with Suppliers and Partners

In the trucking industry, building and maintaining positive relationships with suppliers and partners is crucial to the success of your business. These relationships can include those with truck manufacturers, equipment suppliers, fuel providers, and even other trucking companies. Having strong partnerships with these entities can lead to cost savings, increased efficiency, and a better overall experience for your customers.

When building relationships with suppliers and partners, it is important to be transparent and honest in your communication. This includes clearly outlining your needs and expectations, as well as being open to feedback and suggestions from your partners. It is also important to be prompt in addressing any issues that may arise and to be willing to compromise when necessary.

One key aspect of building positive relationships with suppliers and partners is to establish clear lines of communication. This can include regular check-ins, attending industry events and trade shows, and utilizing technology such as email and messaging apps to stay in touch. This will help to ensure that everyone is on the same page and that any issues can be addressed in a timely manner.

Another important aspect of building positive relationships with suppliers and partners is to be consistent in your business practices. This includes maintaining consistent schedules, being punctual, and following through on your commitments.

This consistency will help to build trust and confidence in your business, making it more likely that your partners will want to continue working with you.

When working with suppliers and partners, it is also important to be mindful of the impact that your business has on the environment. This includes implementing sustainable practices, such as reducing fuel consumption and minimizing waste. Being environmentally conscious can also help to build positive relationships with suppliers and partners, as many companies are now prioritizing sustainable practices.

In summary, building and maintaining positive relationships with suppliers and partners is essential for the success of your trucking business. By being transparent, consistent, and environmentally conscious in your communication and business practices, you can create long-term partnerships that benefit everyone involved.

Establishing and Maintaining Compliance with Safety Regulations

Safety is of the utmost importance in the trucking industry, and as a trucking business owner, it is your responsibility to ensure that your company is in compliance with all federal and state safety regulations. This includes regulations related to driver qualifications, vehicle maintenance, and record keeping.

One of the first steps in establishing compliance with safety regulations is to ensure that all of your drivers meet the qualifications set forth by the Federal Motor Carrier Safety Administration (FMCSA). This includes having a valid commercial driver's license (CDL), passing a physical examination, and completing mandatory training. It is also important to conduct regular background checks and to monitor the driving records of your drivers to ensure that they are in compliance with safety regulations.

Another important aspect of compliance with safety regulations is to maintain your vehicles to the highest standards. This includes regular inspections and maintenance, as well as ensuring that all equipment is in proper working order. The FMCSA also requires that trucking companies keep detailed records of all vehicle maintenance and repairs, so it is important to have a system in place for tracking this information.

In addition to driver qualifications and vehicle maintenance, there are also regulations related to record keeping and reporting. This includes maintaining detailed logs of driver hours of service, as well as reporting any accidents or incidents to the FMCSA. It is important to have a system in place for tracking and reporting this information in order to ensure compliance with regulations.

To maintain compliance with safety regulations, it is also important to stay informed about any changes or updates to the regulations. This can be done by regularly checking the FMCSA website, attending industry events and training sessions, and consulting with industry experts.

In summary, establishing and maintaining compliance with safety regulations is crucial for the success of your trucking business. By ensuring that your drivers meet qualifications, maintaining your vehicles to the highest standards, keeping detailed records, and staying informed about changes to regulations, you can ensure the safety of your drivers, customers, and the general public.

Understanding and Managing Fuel Costs

Fuel is one of the biggest expenses for a trucking business, and it's crucial to have a good understanding of fuel costs in order to effectively manage them. Fuel prices can fluctuate greatly, and it's important to have strategies in place to mitigate the impact of these fluctuations on your business.

One way to manage fuel costs is to monitor fuel prices and plan your routes accordingly. By using websites and apps that track fuel prices, you can choose the most cost-effective routes and plan your trips to take advantage of lower prices. You can also consider using fuel cards or fuel discounts to save money on fuel purchases.

Another way to manage fuel costs is to improve the fuel efficiency of your vehicles. This can be done by implementing regular maintenance and repairs, using lower-viscosity oils, and equipping your vehicles with aerodynamic add-ons. Additionally, by using technology such as GPS, you can reduce idling times, avoid traffic congestion, and optimize your routes which can all lead to better fuel economy.

You can also manage fuel costs by implementing a fuel management program. This can include tracking fuel consumption, monitoring driver behavior, and identifying areas where improvement is needed. By monitoring your fuel consumption and identifying areas where improvements can be made, you can reduce your fuel costs.

Managing fuel costs also includes understanding the tax implications of fuel purchases. The federal government, as well as most states, imposes a tax on fuel purchases, and it is important to understand how this tax applies to your business. Some states offer exemptions or refunds for fuel used in commercial vehicles, so it's important to research and take advantage of any available tax breaks.

In summary, managing fuel costs is a crucial aspect of running a successful trucking business. By monitoring fuel prices, improving fuel efficiency, implementing a fuel management program, and understanding the tax implications of fuel purchases, you can reduce your fuel costs and increase your profitability. Additionally, by staying informed about the latest fuel-saving technologies, you can ensure that your business stays competitive in the long term.

Building and Managing an Effective Dispatch and Routing System

An effective dispatch and routing system is essential for the success of any trucking business. It allows you to efficiently plan and organize your drivers' routes, optimize delivery times, and keep track of your fleet's location and status. In this chapter, we will discuss the key components of a successful dispatch and routing system and provide tips on how to build and manage one for your trucking business.

The first step in building an effective dispatch and routing system is to choose the right software. There are many different types of dispatch software available, each with its own set of features and capabilities. Some popular options include fleet management software, GPS tracking software, and transportation management systems (TMS). When choosing a dispatch software, it's important to consider the specific needs of your business and select a system that can handle those needs.

Once you've selected the right software, it's important to train your staff on how to use it effectively. This includes both your dispatchers and your drivers. Your dispatchers will be responsible for planning routes, scheduling deliveries, and monitoring the status of your fleet. Your drivers will need to know how to use the software to update their location and status, and to access important information such as delivery schedules and route instructions.

Once your staff is trained and your dispatch and routing system is up and running, it's important to regularly review and optimize your routes. This can be done by analyzing data such as delivery times, fuel consumption, and mileage. By identifying areas where you can improve efficiency and reduce costs, you can make adjustments to your routes and improve the overall performance of your business.

Another important aspect of managing a dispatch and routing system is communication. Your dispatchers and drivers need to be able to communicate effectively in order to ensure that deliveries are made on time and that any issues are dealt with promptly. This can be achieved through the use of two-way radios, smartphones, or other communication devices.

In addition to building and managing an effective dispatch and routing system, it's also important to stay current with industry trends and changes. This includes staying informed about new regulations, changes in technology, and the emergence of new competitors. By staying informed and adapting to change, you can ensure that your dispatch and routing system remains competitive and efficient.

In conclusion, an effective dispatch and routing system is crucial to the success of any trucking business. By selecting the right software, training your staff, and regularly optimizing and communicating with your drivers, you can build a system that will help you to efficiently plan and organize your routes, optimize delivery times, and keep track of your fleet's location and status. By staying current with industry trends and changes, you can ensure that your system remains competitive and efficient.

Developing a Marketing Strategy for Your Trucking Business

As a trucking business owner, it's important to have a solid marketing strategy in place to help attract and retain customers. This chapter will provide an overview of key marketing concepts and strategies that can help you grow your business and establish a strong, recognizable brand.

First, it's important to understand your target market. Who are the customers you want to reach and what are their needs? Conducting market research can help you gain insight into the demographics, preferences, and buying habits of your target audience.

Once you have a clear understanding of your target market, you can develop a messaging and positioning strategy that will resonate with them. This could include developing a unique selling proposition (USP) that highlights the benefits of doing business with your company, such as reliability, competitive pricing, or exceptional customer service.

Another key aspect of your marketing strategy should be developing a strong brand identity. This includes creating a logo, tagline, and visual elements that will help customers easily recognize your company and differentiate you from your competitors.

Next, you'll need to choose the appropriate marketing channels to reach your target market. This could include online marketing, such as social media and paid advertising, as well as traditional channels like print and radio advertising, trade shows, and networking events.

As you develop your marketing strategy, it's also important to track your progress and measure the effectiveness of your campaigns. This will help you make data-driven decisions and adjust your strategy as needed to optimize results.

Finally, building and maintaining positive relationships with customers is crucial. By providing exceptional service and going above and beyond to meet their needs, you can earn their loyalty and positive word-of-mouth referrals.

In summary, developing a comprehensive marketing strategy is a critical aspect of building and growing a successful trucking business. By understanding your target market, creating a strong brand identity, and utilizing the right marketing channels, you can attract and retain customers, increase brand awareness, and ultimately drive growth for your company.

Developing a Marketing Strategy for Your Trucking Business

Marketing is an essential aspect of any successful business, and the trucking industry is no exception. A well-crafted marketing strategy can help you attract new customers, retain existing ones, and ultimately grow your business. In this chapter, we will discuss the key components of a marketing strategy for a trucking business and provide some tips on how to implement them effectively.

The first step in developing a marketing strategy is to identify your target market. Who are your ideal customers, and what are their needs and preferences? Are you targeting small businesses, large corporations, or a specific industry? Understanding your target market will help you tailor your marketing efforts to reach the right people.

Once you have identified your target market, you can start developing your marketing mix. The marketing mix consists of four key elements: product, price, place, and promotion.

Product: Your product is the service you provide, which in this case is transportation. Consider how you can differentiate your service from your competitors. Are you offering faster delivery times, more frequent routes, or specialized services?

Price: Pricing is an important consideration for any business, and the trucking industry is no exception. You will need to consider the costs of running your business, as well as the prices charged by your competitors. It is important to find a balance between pricing your services competitively and ensuring that you make a profit.

Place: Place refers to how you distribute your services. In the trucking industry, this might include the routes you operate, the locations you serve, and the methods you use to deliver your services. Consider how you can best reach your target market and what distribution channels will work best for your business.

Promotion: Promotion includes all the activities you use to communicate with your target market and promote your services. This can include advertising, public relations, sales promotions, and personal selling. Consider what methods will be most effective for reaching your target market and budget accordingly.

Once you have developed your marketing mix, you can start implementing your marketing strategy. This may include things like creating a website, advertising in trade publications, attending industry events, and networking with other business owners.

It is also important to track your results and adjust your strategy as needed. Use metrics such as website traffic, customer feedback, and sales figures to measure the effectiveness of your marketing efforts and make adjustments as needed.

In conclusion, a marketing strategy is an essential component of any successful trucking business. By identifying your target market, developing your marketing mix, and implementing your strategy, you can attract new customers, retain existing ones, and ultimately grow your business. Remember to track your results and make adjustments as needed to ensure that your marketing efforts are as effective as possible.

Understanding and Managing Fuel Costs

Fuel costs are one of the biggest expenses for any trucking business. They can also be one of the most unpredictable, as fuel prices fluctuate frequently and can be affected by a number of factors, such as supply and demand, geopolitical events, and weather. It is important for trucking business owners to have a solid understanding of fuel costs and to develop strategies for managing them.

One way to manage fuel costs is to keep track of fuel prices in your area and to plan your routes accordingly. By avoiding areas where fuel prices are high, you can save money on fuel costs. Additionally, you can use tools like fuel price apps or websites to find the cheapest fuel prices in your area.

Another way to manage fuel costs is to invest in fuel-efficient vehicles and equipment. This can include things like aerodynamic trailers and low-rolling-resistance tires, which can help improve fuel economy and reduce fuel costs. Additionally, you can invest in telematics systems, which can provide real-time data on fuel consumption, allowing you to identify and address any issues that may be contributing to high fuel costs.

You can also manage fuel costs by implementing fuel-saving driving techniques, such as avoiding rapid acceleration and braking, and maintaining a steady speed. You can also train your drivers to be mindful of fuel consumption, and encourage them to adopt fuel-efficient driving habits.

It's also important to keep an eye on market prices and trends, and make adjustments to your fuel purchasing and inventory management strategy accordingly. One strategy is to lock in prices with fuel suppliers by signing long-term contracts, which can protect you against sudden price increases.

Finally, you can manage fuel costs by taking advantage of government programs and incentives that are available for fuel-efficient vehicles and equipment.

By understanding and managing fuel costs, trucking business owners can keep this expense in check and improve their bottom line.

Building and Maintaining a Fleet Maintenance Program

One of the most important aspects of running a successful trucking business is having a reliable fleet of vehicles. A well-maintained fleet not only ensures that your trucks are running efficiently and safely, but it can also save you money in the long run by preventing costly breakdowns and repairs. In this chapter, we will discuss how to develop and implement a fleet maintenance program that will help keep your trucks on the road and your business running smoothly.

First and foremost, it is important to establish a regular maintenance schedule for your fleet. This schedule should include routine inspections and maintenance, such as oil changes, tire rotations, and brake inspections, as well as more extensive maintenance, such as engine rebuilds and transmission replacements. It is also important to keep detailed records of all maintenance performed on each vehicle, including the date, type of service, and any parts that were replaced. This information can be used to identify patterns and trends that can help you anticipate future maintenance needs and budget accordingly.

In addition to regular maintenance, it is important to have a plan in place for unexpected repairs and breakdowns. This might include having a list of trusted mechanics and repair shops that you can call on in case of an emergency, as well as a supply of spare parts and tools that you can use to make repairs on the road. Having a plan in place for unexpected repairs can help minimize downtime and keep your trucks on the road, which can be crucial for meeting customer demands and ensuring that your business is profitable.

Another important aspect of maintaining a fleet is ensuring that your vehicles are compliant with all federal and state regulations. This includes meeting emissions standards and passing regular safety inspections. It is also important to stay up-to-date with any changes to regulations, as non-compliance can result in fines and penalties.

Along with routine maintenance and safety compliance, it is essential to have a fleet management system that can help you keep track of all aspects of your fleet, including fuel consumption, maintenance schedules, and driver performance. Many fleet management systems offer real-time data and analytics that can provide insight into how your fleet is performing and help you make data-driven decisions to improve efficiency and reduce costs.

In conclusion, building and maintaining a fleet maintenance program is an essential aspect of running a successful trucking business. It ensures that your vehicles are running efficiently and safely, and it can save you money in the long run by preventing costly breakdowns and repairs. By regularly inspecting and maintaining your vehicles, having a plan in place for unexpected repairs, and staying compliant with regulations, you can keep your trucks on the road and your business running smoothly.

Managing and Reducing Turnover Among Drivers and Staff

One of the biggest challenges facing trucking businesses today is high turnover among drivers and staff. Not only is this costly in terms of recruitment and training, but it can also negatively impact productivity and morale. In this chapter, we will explore some strategies for managing and reducing turnover among drivers and staff.

First, it is important to understand the reasons why drivers and staff may leave your business. Some common reasons include low pay, poor working conditions, lack of opportunities for advancement, and lack of support or recognition. By identifying the root causes of turnover, you can take steps to address these issues and improve retention.

One effective strategy for reducing turnover is to offer competitive pay and benefits. This includes not only offering competitive wages, but also offering benefits such as health insurance, retirement plans, and paid time off. Additionally, it is important to provide regular performance evaluations and opportunities for career advancement.

Another important strategy for reducing turnover is to provide a positive and supportive work environment. This includes providing regular training and development opportunities, fostering open communication and collaboration, and recognizing and rewarding employees for their contributions. Additionally, it is important to ensure that drivers and staff have the necessary resources and support to perform their jobs effectively.

Another strategy to consider is providing a work-life balance for your drivers and staff. This includes providing flexible scheduling, extra time off, and other accommodations to meet the needs of employees. This can help to reduce stress and improve employee satisfaction, which in turn can lead to better retention.

Lastly, effective communication and building a strong relationship with your drivers and staff is key. This means creating an open-door policy, encouraging feedback and suggestions, and making sure they know they are valued members of your team. This can also mean acknowledging their contributions and providing them with opportunities for growth and advancement.

In summary, managing and reducing turnover among drivers and staff is essential for the success of your trucking business. By understanding the reasons why drivers and staff may leave, providing competitive pay and benefits, fostering a positive and supportive work environment, offering flexibility and support, and building strong relationships, you can improve retention and ultimately the success of your business.

Utilizing Social Media and Online Tools to Promote Your Business

In today's digital age, social media and online tools are essential for any business looking to build and maintain a strong online presence. As a trucking business owner, it's important to understand the power of these tools and how to effectively utilize them to promote your business.

First, it's important to establish a strong online presence by creating a professional website and social media accounts on platforms such as Facebook, Twitter, and LinkedIn. These platforms will allow you to connect with potential customers, build relationships with industry partners, and share important information about your business.

Next, consider using online tools such as Google Analytics and social media analytics to track the performance of your online marketing efforts. These tools will provide valuable insights into the effectiveness of your campaigns, allowing you to adjust your strategy as needed.

Consider also using paid online advertising to reach a wider audience. Platforms such as Google AdWords and Facebook Ads allow you to target specific demographics and geographic areas, making it easier to reach potential customers.

In addition, don't underestimate the power of customer reviews and testimonials. Encourage satisfied customers to leave positive reviews on your website and social media accounts, and be sure to respond to any negative feedback in a professional and timely manner.

Finally, stay up-to-date with the latest industry trends and best practices by regularly reading industry publications and participating in online trucking forums and groups. This will not only help you stay current but also give you the opportunity to network with other industry professionals.

By effectively utilizing social media and online tools, you can promote your trucking business and reach new customers, while also building and maintaining a strong online presence.

Understanding and Managing Taxes and Accounting

As a trucking business owner, it's important to understand and stay compliant with all tax and accounting regulations. Failure to do so can result in hefty fines and penalties. In this chapter, we will cover some key areas to focus on when it comes to taxes and accounting for your trucking business.

First and foremost, it's important to keep accurate and detailed records of all financial transactions. This includes income and expenses, as well as any assets and liabilities. This will make it easier for you to prepare and file your taxes, as well as provide a clear picture of the financial health of your business.

Next, you'll need to understand and comply with any tax regulations specific to the trucking industry. This includes taxes on fuel and other operating expenses, as well as taxes on vehicles and equipment. It's important to consult with a tax professional or accountant who is familiar with the trucking industry to ensure you're paying the correct amount of taxes and taking advantage of any deductions or credits that may be available to you.

Another important aspect of taxes and accounting for your trucking business is keeping track of employee taxes and compliance with laws such as the Affordable Care Act and the Federal Motor Carrier Safety Administration. It is important to stay up-to-date on regulations and compliance requirements to avoid any penalties or fines.

Finally, it's important to have a system in place for managing and paying bills, invoices and other financial obligations on time. This will help ensure your business stays financially stable, as well as maintain positive relationships with suppliers and partners.

In summary, taxes and accounting can be a complex and time-consuming aspect of running a trucking business, but it is important to stay compliant and accurate in order to avoid penalties and maintain financial stability. By keeping accurate records, understanding and complying with industry-specific tax regulations, managing employee taxes, and staying up-to-date on regulations, you can ensure that your trucking business is operating in a financially sound manner.

Improving Customer Service and Building a Loyal Customer Base

Starting and running a successful trucking business requires more than just having the right equipment and a team of skilled drivers. It also requires a commitment to providing exceptional customer service. A positive reputation and a loyal customer base are essential for long-term success in this competitive industry.

One of the key elements of providing excellent customer service is understanding your customers' needs and expectations. This means not only delivering on time and on budget, but also being responsive to customer inquiries and addressing any issues that may arise. Building strong, open lines of communication with your customers is key to building trust and fostering a positive relationship.

Another important aspect of customer service is being proactive in addressing potential issues before they become a problem. This could include things like implementing a regular check-in process with customers, or conducting regular surveys to gather feedback on your services. By staying ahead of potential issues, you can quickly address any concerns and maintain a positive relationship with your customers.

In addition to providing great customer service, it's also important to build a loyal customer base. One way to do this is by offering incentives for repeat business, such as discounts or loyalty rewards. You can also build loyalty by consistently delivering high-quality service and going above and beyond to meet the needs of your customers.

Another key to building a loyal customer base is to maintain a strong online presence. Utilizing social media, developing a professional website, and staying active on review sites like Yelp and Google Reviews can all help to improve your online reputation and attract new customers.

Ultimately, providing exceptional customer service and building a loyal customer base takes time, effort, and dedication. But by consistently delivering quality service, building strong relationships with your customers, and staying ahead of potential issues, you can establish a positive reputation and secure a loyal customer base that will help drive your business forward for years to come.

Understanding and Managing Cash Flow and Financial Forecasting

Starting and running a trucking business can be a challenging and complex task, and one of the key factors to success is understanding and managing cash flow and financial forecasting. Cash flow is the movement of money in and out of your business, and it is essential to keep an eye on this to ensure that you have enough money to pay bills, employees, and other expenses. Financial forecasting is the process of looking ahead to predict future financial performance, which can help you make informed decisions about the direction of your business.

When it comes to managing cash flow, there are several strategies you can use to improve this in your trucking business. One is to improve the efficiency of your billing and collections process. This can be done by creating a system that makes it easy to invoice customers promptly, and by following up on unpaid invoices in a timely manner. Another strategy is to reduce expenses and improve profitability. This can be done by implementing cost-saving measures such as reducing fuel consumption, improving driver productivity, and negotiating better rates with suppliers.

Financial forecasting is another important aspect of managing cash flow and can help you identify potential problems before they occur. One of the key elements of forecasting is creating a budget. This will give you a clear picture of what your income and expenses will be in the future, which will help you identify areas where you need to focus your efforts. Additionally, regularly reviewing financial statements and analyzing trends will help you keep an eye on important metrics such as revenues, expenses, and profitability.

Another important aspect of managing cash flow is understanding and managing taxes and accounting. Tax laws and regulations can be complex and ever-changing, so it's important to have a good understanding of the tax laws that apply to your business and to work with a qualified accountant or tax professional. They can help you navigate the tax laws and regulations and ensure that you are paying the correct amount of taxes.

In addition to understanding and managing cash flow and financial forecasting, it's important to have a good understanding of accounting principles. This includes keeping accurate and detailed financial records, reconciling bank statements, and preparing financial statements. This will give you a clear picture of the financial health of your business and help you identify areas where you need to make changes.

In conclusion, understanding and managing cash flow and financial forecasting is a critical aspect of running a successful trucking business. By implementing strategies to improve cash flow and forecasting, you can ensure that your business has the resources it needs to grow and prosper. Additionally, understanding and managing taxes and accounting will help you navigate the complex tax laws and regulations and ensure that you are paying the correct amount of taxes. With the right approach, you can keep your business on track for long-term success.

Developing a Strategy for Recruiting and Retaining Drivers

As a trucking business owner, one of the most important assets you have is your team of drivers. These individuals are responsible for safely and efficiently delivering goods to your customers, and their performance directly impacts the success of your business. However, recruiting and retaining drivers can be a challenge in the competitive trucking industry. In this chapter, we'll discuss strategies for recruiting and retaining drivers to ensure that your business has the talent it needs to thrive.

Recruiting Drivers

The first step in building a strong team of drivers is to attract qualified candidates. There are a number of ways to do this, including:

- Advertising in relevant publications and online job boards
- Partnering with trucking schools and vocational programs
- Offering referral bonuses to current employees
- Participating in job fairs and recruiting events
- Utilizing social media and online recruiting tools

When advertising for driver positions, it's important to highlight the unique benefits of working for your company. For example, you may offer competitive pay and benefits, flexible scheduling, or opportunities for advancement. Additionally, you should be transparent about the qualifications and experience required for the position, as well as the expectations for performance and conduct.

Screening and Hiring Drivers

Once you have a pool of qualified candidates, the next step is to screen and hire the best fit for your business. This process should include:

- Checking references and employment history
- Conducting interviews to assess qualifications and fit
- Administering pre-employment testing, such as drug and alcohol screenings, and physical exams
- Reviewing driving records and motor vehicle reports
- Conducting background checks

Retaining Drivers

Recruiting drivers is an ongoing process, but it's equally important to retain the drivers you already have. High turnover rates can be costly and disruptive to your business. To retain your drivers, consider:

- Offering competitive pay and benefits
- Providing opportunities for advancement and professional development
- Creating a positive and supportive work environment
- Recognizing and rewarding good performance
- Communicating openly and honestly with your drivers
- Being responsive to their needs and concerns

In addition, providing a strong safety culture and training program is essential to retaining drivers. Drivers are more likely to stay with a company that prioritizes their safety, and provides them with the necessary resources and support.

In conclusion, recruiting and retaining drivers is crucial for the success of your trucking business. By utilizing effective recruitment strategies, screening and hiring the best candidates, and creating a positive and supportive work environment, you can build a team of drivers that will help your business thrive.

Building and Maintaining a Safety Culture within Your Company

Safety should always be a top priority for any trucking company. Not only is it important to ensure the well-being of your drivers and staff, but it is also a legal requirement. In addition, maintaining a strong safety culture can lead to lower insurance rates, increased driver retention, and a positive reputation for your business.

One of the most important steps in building a safety culture is to establish clear safety policies and procedures. These should be communicated to all employees and should be easily accessible at all times. It is also important to train employees on these policies and procedures, as well as providing ongoing training to ensure they are up-to-date with the latest regulations and best practices.

In addition to having policies and procedures in place, it is important to have a system in place for reporting and addressing safety incidents. This should include a process for investigating incidents and taking corrective action to prevent them from happening in the future. Regular safety meetings and audits can also be useful in identifying areas where improvements can be made.

Another key aspect of building a safety culture is to actively involve employees in safety efforts. This can include involving them in safety meetings and audits, as well as recognizing and rewarding those who go above and beyond in promoting safety within the company.

It is also important to stay current with federal and state regulations related to safety in the trucking industry. This includes regular compliance audits and updates to policies and procedures as needed to ensure compliance.

In addition to the steps outlined above, there are also a number of other actions that can be taken to promote safety within your company. These include implementing technology such as onboard cameras and GPS tracking, as well as promoting healthy habits such as regular exercise and adequate sleep for drivers.

Overall, building and maintaining a safety culture within your company is essential for the well-being of your employees and for the success of your business. By establishing clear policies and procedures, involving employees in safety efforts, staying current with regulations, and taking a proactive approach to addressing and preventing incidents, you can create a culture of safety that will benefit everyone involved.

Navigating the Legal Landscape of the Trucking Industry

Starting and running a trucking business can be a challenging task, and one aspect that is often overlooked is the legal landscape of the industry. However, understanding and complying with federal and state regulations is crucial for the success of your business. In this chapter, we will explore the various legal considerations you should keep in mind as a trucking business owner.

Federal Regulations

The Federal Motor Carrier Safety Administration (FMCSA) is the main regulatory body for the trucking industry at the federal level. They are responsible for enforcing safety regulations and standards for commercial motor vehicles. Some of the key regulations you will need to comply with include:

- Hours of Service (HOS) regulations: These regulations dictate the maximum number of hours a driver can operate a commercial motor vehicle in a given period. Drivers must take a break after a certain number of hours on the road and keep detailed logs of their HOS.
- Drug and alcohol testing: Drivers are subject to random drug and alcohol testing. Additionally, all new hires must be tested before they begin driving.
- Vehicle maintenance: Your vehicles must be kept in good working order, with regular inspections and maintenance.

- Insurance: All commercial motor vehicles must be insured to a minimum level.
- Driver qualifications: All drivers must be properly licensed and meet certain qualifications, such as being at least 21 years old and passing a physical examination.

State Regulations

In addition to federal regulations, each state also has its own set of regulations that you must comply with. Some states have stricter regulations than others, so it is important to be familiar with the regulations in the states where you operate. Some common state regulations include:

- Weight and size restrictions: Some states have restrictions on the weight and size of vehicles that can operate on their roads.
- IFTA: The International Fuel Tax Agreement (IFTA) is a fuel tax program that allows commercial motor vehicles to report and pay fuel taxes to their base state instead of every state they operate in.
- IRP: The International Registration Plan (IRP) is a program that allows commercial motor vehicles to register with their base state instead of every state they operate in.
- UCR: The Unified Carrier Registration (UCR) is a program that requires trucking companies to register and pay an annual fee based on the number of commercial motor vehicles they operate.
- Permits: Some states require special permits for certain types of loads or vehicles.

It's important to note that regulations are subject to change and new regulations may be added. It is the responsibility of the trucking business to stay up to date and comply with all federal and state regulations.

Legal Compliance

Compliance with legal regulations is not only important to avoid penalties and fines, but it also helps to keep your drivers and the public safe. The trucking industry is heavily regulated, and it is essential to have a compliance management system in place to ensure that you are meeting all of the legal requirements. This includes maintaining accurate records, performing regular safety audits, and having a process for addressing violations.

In addition to complying with regulations, it is also important to have a good working relationship with legal counsel. A good attorney can help you navigate the legal landscape and advise you on any potential legal issues that may arise.

One of the most important federal regulations that trucking companies must comply with is the Federal Motor Carrier Safety Administration (FMCSA) regulations. These regulations cover a wide range of topics, including driver qualifications, vehicle maintenance, and recordkeeping. For example, the FMCSA requires that all commercial drivers have a valid commercial driver's license (CDL) and meet certain qualifications such as passing a physical examination and drug and alcohol testing. Additionally, the FMCSA requires that all vehicles used in commercial transportation be regularly inspected and maintained to ensure that they are in safe operating condition.

In addition to the FMCSA regulations, trucking companies must also comply with state regulations. These regulations can vary widely from state to state, so it is important to understand the specific laws and regulations that apply to your business. For example, some states have stricter requirements for commercial vehicle inspections and maintenance than others. Additionally, some states have specific regulations regarding the transportation of hazardous materials, which can impact your business if you transport these types of materials.

To ensure compliance with federal and state regulations, it is important to have a clear understanding of the laws and regulations that apply to your business, as well as to have systems and procedures in place to ensure that you are in compliance. This may include regular vehicle inspections and maintenance, maintaining accurate records, and providing regular training to your drivers and staff.

Another important legal aspect of the trucking industry is insurance and liability. As a trucking business owner, you are responsible for ensuring that your vehicles and drivers are properly insured. This includes liability insurance to protect against third-party claims resulting from accidents or injuries caused by your vehicles or drivers. Additionally, you may need to have cargo insurance to protect against losses or damage to the goods that you transport. It is important to review your insurance coverage regularly and to ensure that it is adequate to protect your business from potential financial losses.

In addition to insurance and liability, there are a variety of other legal issues that trucking companies must navigate, including labor laws, contract law, and compliance with environmental regulations. It is important to work with an attorney who is knowledgeable about the trucking industry and can provide guidance and advice on these and other legal issues that may arise.

In conclusion, navigating the legal landscape of the trucking industry can be challenging, but with a clear understanding of the laws and regulations that apply to your business, as well as the right systems and procedures in place, you can protect your business from potential legal issues and ensure compliance with federal and state regulations. Additionally, working with an attorney who is knowledgeable about the trucking industry can provide valuable guidance and advice on legal matters and help you navigate the legal landscape of the trucking industry.

Utilizing Telematics and Other Technology to Improve Productivity

Technology is rapidly changing the trucking industry and it's important for business owners to stay up to date on the latest tools and technologies to improve efficiency and productivity. One such technology that is becoming increasingly popular in the industry is telematics.

Telematics is the use of GPS and other technologies to track and monitor the performance of a vehicle or fleet. This information can be used to improve routing, reduce fuel consumption, and improve overall fleet performance. Some examples of telematics technology include:

- GPS tracking: This allows you to track the location and movement of your vehicles in real-time. This information can be used to improve routing and reduce fuel consumption.
- Electronic logging devices (ELDs): These devices are required by the Federal Motor Carrier Safety Administration (FMCSA) for commercial vehicles and help ensure compliance with hours-of-service regulations.
- Vehicle diagnostics: This technology allows you to monitor the performance of your vehicles and identify potential issues before they become major problems.
- Driver behavior monitoring: This technology allows you to monitor the behavior of your drivers and identify any potential safety concerns.

In addition to telematics, there are many other technologies that can help improve productivity in your trucking business. Some examples include:

- Automated dispatching: This technology allows you to automate the dispatching process and improve communication with your drivers.
- Transportation management systems (TMS): These systems help you manage your logistics and operations, including routing, scheduling, and tracking.
- Mobile apps: Many companies are developing mobile apps for their drivers and staff to improve communication and increase efficiency.
- Artificial intelligence (AI) and machine learning: These technologies can be used to analyze data and make predictions about future demand, helping you to better plan and manage your operations.

When implementing new technologies in your business, it's important to consider the cost, the level of integration with your existing systems, and the potential return on investment. It's also important to provide training for your staff to ensure they are able to effectively use the new technologies.

In conclusion, technology can play a vital role in improving the productivity of your trucking business. Telematics and other technologies can help you reduce costs, improve safety, and increase efficiency. As the industry continues to evolve, it's important to stay up to date on the latest tools and technologies and implement those that make sense for your business.

Building and maintaining relationships with other businesses in the supply chain

Introduction

In the trucking industry, building and maintaining positive relationships with other businesses in the supply chain is essential for success. These relationships can include partnerships with freight brokers, shippers, and other carriers, as well as relationships with suppliers of goods and services. By developing strong partnerships and working closely with other businesses in the supply chain, trucking companies can improve their efficiency, reduce costs, and gain a competitive advantage.

Why relationships matter

In the trucking industry, relationships with other businesses in the supply chain can play a critical role in determining a company's success. For example, a strong relationship with a freight broker can lead to consistent, high-volume shipments, while a positive relationship with a shipper can ensure that a company is the first choice for hauling their goods. Additionally, partnerships with other carriers can help a company expand their reach and gain access to new markets.

On the supply side, building positive relationships with suppliers of goods and services can lead to better prices and faster delivery times. This can be especially important for trucking companies, as fuel, tires, and maintenance can be major expenses. By working closely with suppliers, trucking companies can negotiate better deals and ensure that they have the resources they need to keep their fleet on the road.

Developing relationships

Developing positive relationships with other businesses in the supply chain can take time and effort, but it is worth it in the long run. One of the most important things to remember is that relationships are built on trust and mutual benefit. This means that trucking companies need to be reliable, professional, and responsive to the needs of their partners.

One way to build trust is to consistently deliver high-quality service. This means being on time, communicating effectively, and providing detailed and accurate information about shipments. Additionally, it's important to be responsive to the needs of partners and to be willing to work together to solve problems.

Another key aspect of developing relationships is being open to new opportunities. This means being willing to take on new types of shipments, working with new partners, and exploring new markets. By being open to new opportunities, trucking companies can build a diverse portfolio of partners and customers, which can help to reduce risk and increase revenue.

Managing relationships

Once relationships have been established, it's important to actively manage and maintain them. This means regularly communicating with partners and customers, keeping them updated on the status of shipments, and addressing any issues that arise. Additionally, it's important to keep partners and customers informed of any changes or updates to company policies or procedures.

It's also essential to be responsive to the needs of partners and customers, even when things don't go as planned. This means being willing to work together to resolve issues, whether they are related to a specific shipment or a more general problem. By being responsive and proactive, trucking companies can build a reputation for dependability and reliability.

Conclusion

Building and maintaining positive relationships with other businesses in the supply chain is essential for success in the trucking industry. By developing strong partnerships and working closely with other businesses, trucking companies can improve their efficiency, reduce costs, and gain a competitive advantage. Additionally, by actively managing relationships and being responsive to the needs of partners and customers, trucking companies can build a reputation for dependability and reliability, which can be key to long-term success in the industry.

Understanding the Role of Freight Brokers and How to Work With Them

Introduction: As a trucking business owner, it's important to understand the role of freight brokers and how they can be beneficial to your business. Freight brokers are intermediaries between shippers and carriers, and they can help connect you with new customers and opportunities for freight transportation. However, it's important to have a clear understanding of how to work with freight brokers and the legal requirements that come with it. In this chapter, we will cover the basics of what freight brokers do, how to find the right freight broker for your business, and how to maintain a successful partnership with them.

What do freight brokers do? Freight brokers act as intermediaries between shippers (the companies or individuals who need to transport goods) and carriers (the trucking companies that transport the goods). They are responsible for finding and coordinating transportation for shippers, and they often work with a network of carriers to find the best match for each shipment. Brokers typically handle the negotiation of rates and terms, and they often handle the logistics of the shipment, such as tracking and communication with the carrier.

Finding the right freight broker: When looking for a freight broker, it's important to find one that is reputable and has experience in your specific industry. You can ask for references from other trucking companies, or check out online directories and review websites. It's also a good idea to look for brokers that are licensed by the Federal Motor Carrier Safety

Administration (FMCSA) and have a good standing with the Better Business Bureau (BBB).

Maintaining a successful partnership: Once you've found the right freight broker, it's important to establish clear lines of communication and open up a dialogue about your expectations and needs. This can help ensure a smooth and successful partnership. It's also important to make sure that the broker fully understands your business and the specific types of freight you are willing to haul. Additionally, it's important to be aware of the legal requirements when working with freight brokers, such as the requirement for broker bonds and the need to comply with FMCSA regulations.

Benefits of working with freight brokers: Working with freight brokers can provide many benefits for your trucking business. They can help you find new customers and opportunities for freight transportation, which can increase your revenue and grow your business. They can also help you find the right match for each shipment, which can save you time and resources by reducing the need for empty backhauls. Additionally, freight brokers can handle many of the logistics of the shipment, such as tracking and communication with the carrier, which can free up time for you to focus on other aspects of your business.

Conclusion: Understanding the role of freight brokers and how to work with them is an important aspect of running a successful trucking business. By finding the right freight broker, maintaining clear lines of communication, and understanding the legal requirements, you can build a successful partnership that can help grow your business and increase your revenue. With the benefits that freight brokers can bring, it's well worth the effort to understand how to work with them effectively.

Mastering Negotiation and Pricing Strategies

As a business owner in the trucking industry, it is important to have a solid understanding of negotiation and pricing strategies. These skills can help you secure profitable contracts, build strong relationships with clients and partners, and ultimately, drive the growth and success of your business.

Negotiation is the process of reaching an agreement between two or more parties. In the trucking industry, this often involves negotiating with clients and partners to determine the terms of a contract or agreement. It is important to approach negotiations with a clear understanding of your own goals and the goals of the other party. This can help you to identify areas of common ground and develop creative solutions that benefit all parties involved.

When it comes to pricing, it is important to understand the costs associated with providing your services. This includes not only the cost of fuel, maintenance, and labor, but also any additional costs such as permits, tolls, and compliance with regulations. Once you have a clear understanding of these costs, you can then develop a pricing strategy that allows you to remain competitive while still earning a profit.

One effective pricing strategy is to offer a range of pricing options to clients. For example, you could offer a lower rate for a longer-term contract, or a higher rate for a shorter-term contract. This allows clients to choose a pricing option that best fits their needs and budget.

Another important factor to consider when developing a pricing strategy is your competition. It is important to stay informed about the rates and services offered by other trucking companies in your area. This can help you to adjust your pricing accordingly and remain competitive.

In addition to traditional negotiations and pricing strategies, technology has also played a key role in the trucking industry. Platforms such as Uber Freight, DAT and TMS allow shippers and carriers to negotiate and lock in prices in real-time, with a high degree of transparency, this is something to consider as well.

In order to be successful in the trucking industry, it is important to master the art of negotiation and pricing. By understanding your own costs and the needs of your clients and partners, you can develop strategies that help you to secure profitable contracts and build strong, long-lasting relationships. And don't forget to stay updated with the new technologies and market trends, as they can give you an edge in the industry.

Understanding and managing fuel costs

Fuel costs are one of the largest expenses that trucking businesses must manage, and they can have a significant impact on the profitability of a business. In order to effectively manage fuel costs, it is important to understand the factors that influence fuel prices, as well as the various strategies that can be used to reduce fuel consumption and costs.

Factors That Influence Fuel Prices

Fuel prices are influenced by a variety of factors, including global oil production and demand, geopolitical events, and taxes and regulations. For example, when oil production is high and demand is low, fuel prices tend to be lower, while when production is low and demand is high, fuel prices tend to be higher. Additionally, geopolitical events such as conflicts in oil-producing countries or natural disasters can disrupt oil production and lead to higher prices. Finally, taxes and regulations can also play a role, as governments may impose taxes on fuel or regulate its production and distribution.

Strategies for Reducing Fuel Consumption and Costs

There are several strategies that trucking businesses can use to reduce fuel consumption and costs, including:

- Improving vehicle fuel efficiency: One of the most effective ways to reduce fuel consumption and costs is to improve the fuel efficiency of the vehicles in your fleet. This can be achieved through a variety of means, including using more fuel-efficient engines, optimizing vehicle aerodynamics, and reducing vehicle weight.

- Route optimization: Another way to reduce fuel consumption and costs is to optimize routes. By using software tools, trucking businesses can plan the most efficient routes for their drivers to take, which can help reduce fuel consumption and costs.
- Driver training: In addition to improving vehicle fuel efficiency and optimizing routes, trucking businesses can also reduce fuel consumption and costs by training drivers to drive more efficiently. This can include teaching them about the effects of speeding, idling, and braking on fuel consumption, as well as encouraging them to take advantage of fuel-saving technologies such as cruise control.
- Fuel purchasing: Finally, trucking businesses can also reduce fuel consumption and costs by purchasing fuel at the right time and at the right price. This can include taking advantage of fuel discounts or loyalty programs, as well as purchasing fuel when prices are low.

By understanding the factors that influence fuel prices and implementing strategies to reduce fuel consumption and costs, trucking businesses can better manage their fuel expenses and improve their bottom line.

In addition to these strategies, it is also important to monitor fuel costs on a regular basis to identify patterns and trends. This can help trucking businesses anticipate changes in fuel prices and adjust their operations accordingly. It can also be helpful to compare the prices of different fuel providers, and negotiate with them for better deals.

Another important aspect of managing fuel costs is to maintain accurate and detailed records of fuel purchases, consumption and expenses. This information can be used to monitor the performance of the fleet, identify problem areas and make adjustments to improve fuel efficiency.

In conclusion, managing fuel costs is an ongoing process that requires ongoing attention and monitoring. By understanding the factors that influence fuel prices, implementing strategies to reduce fuel consumption and costs, and monitoring fuel costs regularly, trucking businesses can better control their fuel expenses and improve their bottom line.

Building and Maintaining a Culture of Continuous Improvement

As a trucking business owner or manager, it is important to constantly strive for improvement in all aspects of your operations. This includes not only your bottom line, but also the safety and satisfaction of your drivers and staff, the quality of your service, and your impact on the environment and community. One way to achieve this is by building and maintaining a culture of continuous improvement within your company.

A culture of continuous improvement is one in which all employees, from the top down, are committed to identifying and implementing changes that will make the company better. This can be achieved in a number of ways, such as:

1. Encouraging employee feedback and ideas: One of the best ways to identify areas for improvement is by listening to the people who are on the front lines of your operations. Encourage your employees to share their ideas and concerns, and make sure they feel heard and valued.
2. Implementing a continuous improvement program: A formal continuous improvement program can help you identify areas for improvement, prioritize and track changes, and measure the results. This can include tools like Six Sigma, Lean Manufacturing, or Total Quality Management.
3. Providing training and development opportunities: Investing in the skills and knowledge of your employees can lead to increased productivity, improved quality, and reduced costs. By providing ongoing training and

development opportunities, you can help your employees grow and improve as individuals and as a team.

4. Recognizing and rewarding improvement: Recognizing and rewarding employees for their contributions to continuous improvement can help foster a culture of engagement and motivation. This can be done through bonuses, promotions, or other forms of recognition.

5. Celebrating successes: It's important to celebrate successes and improvements, big or small. This helps to build morale and a sense of accomplishment among your employees, and helps everyone to see the tangible results of their efforts.

By building and maintaining a culture of continuous improvement, you can keep your trucking business on the cutting edge of technology, safety, and customer service, and position it for long-term success.

One way to achieve this is by implementing a telematics system, which can help you track and improve a variety of aspects of your operations, such as fuel efficiency, driver behavior, and vehicle maintenance. By using data and analytics to identify areas for improvement, and then making changes based on that information, you can improve the overall performance of your fleet.

Another way to improve your operations is by building and maintaining positive relationships with other businesses in the supply chain, such as shippers, receivers, and other carriers. By working together and sharing information, you can improve the efficiency of your operations, reduce costs, and provide better service to your customers.

Finally, understanding the role of freight brokers and how to work with them can also help you to improve your business. Freight brokers can help you to find loads and negotiate rates, but it's important to work with reputable and reliable brokers. By building and maintaining good relationships with brokers, you can ensure a steady stream of work for your fleet.

In conclusion, building and maintaining a culture of continuous improvement is essential for the long-term success of your trucking business. By encouraging employee feedback and ideas, implementing a continuous improvement program, providing training and development opportunities, recognizing and rewarding improvement, and celebrating successes, you can foster a culture of engagement and motivation that will help your business to excel. Additionally, utilizing technology such as telematics, building and maintaining relationships with other businesses in the supply chain, and understanding the role of freight brokers can also help you to improve your operations, reduce costs, and provide better service to your customers.

Managing and Reducing Downtime and Lost Productivity

As a trucking business owner, it's important to understand that downtime and lost productivity can have a significant impact on your bottom line. Downtime can be caused by a variety of factors such as equipment breakdowns, driver shortages, and poor route planning. It's essential to have strategies in place to manage and reduce downtime to keep your business running smoothly and efficiently.

One way to manage and reduce downtime is by implementing a preventative maintenance program. This involves regularly scheduled maintenance on your equipment to keep it in good working condition and reduce the likelihood of breakdowns. This could include regular oil changes, tire rotations, and inspections of all mechanical and electrical systems. By proactively maintaining your equipment, you can reduce the likelihood of breakdowns and prolong the life of your equipment.

Another strategy for reducing downtime is to invest in technology that can help you track and manage your fleet in real-time. Telematics systems, for example, allow you to track your vehicles' location, speed, and fuel consumption, which can help you optimize routes, reduce fuel costs, and improve safety.

Driver shortages can also cause downtime and lost productivity. To address this, it's important to have a strategy for recruiting and retaining drivers. This could include offering competitive pay and benefits, providing training and development opportunities, and creating a positive and supportive work culture.

Finally, to reduce downtime, it's essential to have a good routing and dispatch system in place. This means planning routes that are both efficient and safe, taking into account factors such as traffic, weather, and road conditions. It's also important to have a system in place for managing and communicating with drivers to ensure that they are on schedule and aware of any changes or delays.

In summary, managing and reducing downtime and lost productivity is essential to running a successful trucking business. By implementing a preventative maintenance program, investing in technology, recruiting and retaining drivers, and having a good routing and dispatch system in place, you can keep your business running smoothly and efficiently.

Understanding and managing employee benefits and payroll

Managing employee benefits and payroll can be a challenging task for any business, but it is especially important in the trucking industry where the workforce is made up of mostly long-distance truck drivers. In this chapter, we will discuss the importance of employee benefits and payroll in the trucking industry, and provide tips for managing these areas effectively.

The Importance of Employee Benefits and Payroll in the Trucking Industry

Employee benefits and payroll are critical to the success of any business, but they are especially important in the trucking industry. Long-distance truck drivers spend most of their time on the road, away from their families and homes. This can be a difficult lifestyle, and providing a comprehensive benefits package can help to attract and retain top talent. Additionally, payroll is an important aspect of any business, but it is especially important in the trucking industry where drivers are paid by the mile.

Tips for Managing Employee Benefits and Payroll

1. Understand the legal requirements: It is important to understand the legal requirements for employee benefits and payroll in your state and federal laws. This will help you to ensure that you are providing the right benefits and paying your employees accurately and on time.
2. Communicate effectively: Communication is key when it comes to managing employee benefits and payroll.

Make sure that your employees understand their benefits and how they are paid. This will help to prevent misunderstandings and ensure that your employees are satisfied with their benefits and pay.

3. Keep accurate records: Keeping accurate records is essential for managing employee benefits and payroll. This will help you to track employee hours and pay, and ensure that you are providing the correct benefits to your employees.

4. Be flexible: Be open to the needs and preferences of your employees when it comes to benefits and pay. Some drivers may prefer more vacation time, while others may prefer a higher salary. Being flexible will help you to attract and retain top talent.

5. Use technology: There are many software programs available that can help you to manage employee benefits and payroll. Utilize these tools to streamline your processes and make your job easier.

In conclusion, managing employee benefits and payroll is critical to the success of any business, but it is especially important in the trucking industry. By understanding the legal requirements, communicating effectively, keeping accurate records, being flexible and utilizing technology, you can effectively manage employee benefits and payroll, attract and retain top talent, and ensure that your business runs smoothly.

Planning for the Future: Continual Growth and Expansion of Your Trucking Business

As a trucking business owner, it is important to have a clear vision for the future of your company. This includes not only short-term goals, such as increasing revenue or reducing expenses, but also long-term plans for growth and expansion. In order to achieve these goals, it is essential to have a solid understanding of the trucking industry and the potential opportunities and challenges that lie ahead.

One key aspect of planning for the future is staying current with industry trends and changes. This includes staying informed about new regulations, technological advancements, and shifts in consumer demand. For example, changes in fuel prices and emissions standards can have a major impact on your business, so it is important to be aware of these issues and plan accordingly. Additionally, staying current with industry trends can help you identify new opportunities for growth, such as expanding into new markets or offering new services.

Another important aspect of planning for the future is developing a strategy for recruiting and retaining drivers. As the trucking industry continues to evolve, the demand for skilled drivers is expected to increase. To meet this demand, you will need to have a plan in place for recruiting and retaining high-quality drivers. This may involve offering competitive compensation packages, providing ongoing training and development opportunities, or implementing a mentorship program.

In addition to staying current with industry trends and recruiting top-quality drivers, it is also essential to have a solid financial plan in place. This includes understanding and managing cash flow and financial forecasting, as well as developing a budget and setting financial goals. It is also important to have a good understanding of taxes and accounting, so that you can accurately track your income and expenses and make informed business decisions.

Another important aspect of planning for the future is building and maintaining positive relationships with suppliers and partners. Strong partnerships with other businesses in the supply chain can help you achieve cost savings, improve efficiency, and increase revenue. Additionally, working closely with freight brokers can help you expand your business and reach new customers.

Finally, it is essential to have a culture of continuous improvement within your company. This means constantly looking for ways to improve processes, increase productivity, and reduce costs. Additionally, it is important to create a culture that encourages open communication, teamwork, and the sharing of ideas. By fostering a culture of continuous improvement, you will be better positioned to adapt to changes in the industry and take advantage of new opportunities for growth and expansion.

In conclusion, planning for the future of your trucking business requires staying current with industry trends, developing a strategy for recruiting and retaining drivers, having a solid financial plan in place, building and maintaining positive relationships with suppliers and partners, and fostering a culture of continuous improvement. By taking the time to plan ahead, you will be better equipped to navigate the challenges and opportunities of the trucking industry and achieve long-term success.

In conclusion, running a successful trucking business requires a diverse set of skills and knowledge. From understanding and managing fuel costs, to building and maintaining a fleet maintenance program, to developing a marketing strategy, and planning for the future, it takes a lot of hard work, dedication, and perseverance to make it in the trucking industry. But with the right mindset, a solid plan, and a team of skilled and motivated individuals, you can achieve success and take your business to the next level.

As you navigate the challenges of running a trucking business, remember to stay current with industry trends and changes, stay compliant with safety regulations, and always strive to improve your operations. Building and maintaining positive relationships with suppliers and partners, as well as your customers, is key to success. And, perhaps most importantly, building and maintaining a culture of continuous improvement will help you identify and capitalize on new opportunities, and stay ahead of the competition.

We hope this book has been a valuable resource for you, and that the tips, strategies, and advice shared here will help you grow and thrive in the trucking industry. Best of luck to you as you continue to build and grow your business. We wish you all the success and prosperity for your trucking business.